Prosperity
of
the
Soul

by

Jerry Savelle

HARRISON HOUSE
P.O. Box 35035
Tulsa, Okla. 74135

Unless otherwise indicated. all Scripture quotations in this volume are from the *King James Version of the Bible.*

Scripture quotations are from the Amplified New Testament, © The Lockman Foundation 1954, 1958 and are used by permission.

ISBN 0-89274-135-4
Printed in the United States of America

CONTENTS

1
A Citizen Of The Kingdom

"Beloved, I wish above all things that thou mayest prosper and be in health, even as thy soul prospereth. I have no greater joy than to hear that my children walk in truth. Beloved, follow not that which is evil, but that which is good. He that doeth good is of God: but he that doeth evil hath not seen God" (3 John 2,4,11). To whom is John speaking when the Spirit of God prompts him to say "Beloved"? Are you one of the beloved? If you are, can you, as an individual, have prosperity? Before you begin the study of prosperity you need to become totally established in the fact that prosperity is the will of God. Prosperity is for you; however, there are conditions that you have to meet.

Verse 2 in the above Scripture passage says, "Beloved, I wish above all things that thou mayest prosper and be in health, even as thy soul prospereth." My Bible cross reference put it this way: "Beloved, I pray, or *I desire* above all things that thou mayest prosper . . . ." The "*thou*" that He is talking to is *the beloved*. Whoever the beloved is that he was talking to in that epistle stands good, firm, and true anywhere the word "beloved" is found in the Word of God.

If you are a Christian, you are *one of the beloved.* And if you are not *one of the beloved,* Jesus made it easy for you to become *one.* Just do what Paul tells you to do in Romans 10:9 and you will become *one of the beloved.* "That if thou shalt confess with thy mouth the Lord Jesus, and shalt believe in thine heart that God hath raised him from the dead, thou shalt be saved."

John is talking to the beloved, and he is saying, "Beloved, I desire above *all things* . . . ." ALL THINGS: not *some things;* not *many things,* but *all things.* "I desire — I pray above *all things* . . . ." Evidently, this has priority with God. And if it has priority with Him it has priority with me.

Somebody said, "Well, He is only talking about spiritual prosperity. God doesn't want us to have anything that isn't spiritual."

If you say that, you haven't read your Bible very thoroughly! The Bible says that God has already blessed us with *all* spiritual blessings, and made us to sit together in heavenly places in Christ Jesus (See Ephesians 1:3, 20; 2:6; 3:10). However, He has not only blessed us with spiritual things, but the Apostle Peter said that He has obtained for us all things that pertain to LIFE AND GODLINESS. God wants us to be blessed in every area of our lives.

WHEN I BECAME ONE OF THE BELOVED

I was raised in a denominational church, and I went to church every Sunday. But I heard very little that was preached. I am not proud of my actions, but after I did receive the Lord, I was glad that I didn't have a lot of religious tradition to unlearn. I had the idea that God's Word was a story book — beautiful stories about what happened to men a long time ago. I had no earthly idea that the Bible could be applied to one's life today.

Since I didn't know very much about the Bible, I thought I wasn't supposed to pray for material things and I didn't dare pray for any kind of financial blessing. I thought the only thing to ask God for was something spiritual.

I thought, "Well, if the only things I can talk to God about are spiritual, then I have nothing to say to Him". I did not bother communicating with Him until one day when I was still in high school. I decided that I wanted to become a great track star, a pole-vaulter. I would sit around and think about all of the records that I was going to break. I just knew I could do it! I remembered hearing somebody tell about how they had prayed and asked God for something. I decided that, since I was going to be a great track star, maybe I should talk to God about it. That is the only time that I can remember that I really prayed when I was growing up. I knelt down beside my bed and said, "God, if You'll make me a great pole-vaulter and help me break all those records, then I will serve You; I'll turn my life over to You." I really thought that I was offering Him a pretty good deal!

The next day at track practice I broke my leg on the very first attempt. I thought, "Bless God! That's the last time I'll ever ask Him for anything." The kind of image that I had of God was that I shouldn't dare ask Him for anything that has to do with the material realm or the financial realm. The only thing I could talk to God about was something spiritual, and the only people who reach Him are those who talk spiritual. So, I grew up with the idea that I was not supposed to ask God to bless me financially or materially. The only thing that I could talk to God about was something spiritual, like getting saved and going to Heaven.

I FOUND THE KEY!

It was very startling to me to find that the Word of God says, ". . . I pray (desire, wish) above all things that thou mayest prosper and be in health even as your soul prospers." I had never heard anybody say anything like that before.

I thought, "Dear Lord! Either I have not heard the truth or the apostle John is wrong." John wrote by the inspiration of the Holy Spirit. The Word of God is forever settled in heaven. It is eternal! The Bible says that the grass withers and the flower fades, but the Word of God shall stand forever. I chose to believe what the Word said. This led me to believe that maybe God was interested in my financial, physical, and material welfare.

I also began to realize that I could surely get off into an area of danger, if I began to magnify the wrong things. If I got my eyes on money or on things, I could miss the whole point of what He is saying here. I read some more. Jesus said in Matthew 6:24 "No man can serve two masters: for either he will hate the one, and love the other; or else he will hold to the one, and despise the other. Ye cannot serve God and mammon." And "Therefore I say unto you, take no thought for your life, what ye shall eat, or what ye shall drink; nor yet for your body, what ye shall put on. Is not the life more than meat, and the body than raiment?" (v.25) I read, ". . . Your heavenly Father knoweth that ye have need of all these things. But seek ye first the kingdom of God, and His righteousness; and all these things shall be added unto you" (vv. 32,33). I also read what Jesus said in Luke chapter 12. I liked what I found in verse 32: "Fear not, little flock; for it is your Fathers good pleasure to give you the kingdom." I had to *dig deeper* into the Word. I read those verses again. ". . . all of these things shall be added . . ." What other things? I backed up and reread this passage of scripture. I then realized that if I would seek FIRST the kingdom of God, and HIS RIGHTEOUSNESS, then, thank God, He would supply all the material necessities of life: my food, clothing, shelter, and drink.

I said, "Well! Praise God! That must be the key. I have to FIRST seek the kingdom of God. But how can I go about seeking FIRST the kingdom?" I kept on reading the Word and I discovered that through the substitutionary sacrifice of Jesus, according to Colossians, Ephesians, Galatians, and all of Paul's epistles, that He has already delivered us from the power of darkness, and translated us into the kingdom of His dear Son. I realized that first I had to seek the kingdom of God, then I would enter into that kingdom through the *new birth*. I was born again, praise God, *and through the new birth I entered into the kingdom of God. I became one of the beloved!*

"OH, BUT THAT DOESN'T MAKE YOU RIGHTEOUS." SOMEONE SAID

I accepted the fact that because — I WAS BORN AGAIN, I was no longer in the power of darkness. I had been translated into the kingdom of God through the new birth. And *I thought*, "That's one down, and one to go, now all I have to do is seek His righteousness."

I was confused, because Spirit filled, tongue talking, Bible carrying, Church going, Christians had told me, "Brother, you will never be righteous until you get to heaven."

I decided that if I couldn't become righteous until I get to heaven, then I couldn't expect any kind of material blessing until I get to heaven, because He said, "Seek ye first the kingdom and His righteousness, *then* all these things shall be added unto you."

I thought, "Dear Lord! I'm not going to need those things when I get to heaven. I need them now! And if I can't get them until I become righteous, then I am wasting my time down here asking You to bless me."

As I studied the Word, I found out that we do not become righteous when we get to heaven. In fact, unless we become righteous while we are here on the earth, we won't go to heaven. The Bible says in Romans 10:9-10, "That if thou shalt confess with thy mouth the Lord Jesus, and shalt believe in thine heart that God hath raised him from the dead, thou shalt be saved. For with the heart man believeth unto righteousness; and with the mouth confession is made unto salvation." Romans 5:17 says, "For if by one man's offence death reigned by one; much more they which receive abundance of grace and of *the gift of righteousness* shall reign in life by one, Jesus Christ." Righteousness if a gift! Romans 3:22 says, ". . . the righteousness of God which is by faith of Jesus Christ unto all and upon all them that believe. . ." Righteousness is received by faith and verse 25 tells us that we are to declare Jesus' righteousness.

I saw the light! I did seek the kingdom of God. *I did seek HIS righteousness. I believed in my heart that I had been made the righteousness of God: I received it by faith.* And you know what happened? All of those "other things" started coming in, just as He said. Why? Because they belong to me. God promised them in His Word.

YOU CAN HAVE IT TOO!

When you *accept Jesus as the Lord of your life,* you *become a citizen of the kingdom of God.* You become a joint-heir with Jesus; and heir of God; delivered from the power of darkness, and translated into the kingdom of God. You become *one of the beloved!* Then you are ready to receive the *prosperity that is rightfully yours.*

2
Jesus Paid the Same Price For It All

As we look at the subject of prosperity, we are going to look at it from perhaps a different angle than you have considered it before. We are going to talk about *Prosperity of the Soul.* And when you finish this study, you will be able to see what can be produced as a result of your soul prospering. We will read again: "Beloved, I wish above all things that thou mayest prosper and be in health, even as thy soul prospereth. I have no greater joy than to hear that my children walk in truth. Beloved, follow not that which is evil, but that which is good. He that doeth good is of God: but he that doeth evil hath not seen God" (3 John 2, 4, 11). Please note: I am not trying to take Scriptures out of context. My main purpose in skipping around is for the sake of space.

Somebody said, "Well, that was written to only one individual." Well, if it were, He shouldn't have put it in my Bible. I am one of the beloved, and as far as I am concerned, He wrote that letter to you and me. If you think differently don't tell me about it! Because it is working for me. If He is talking to *one beloved,* He is talking to all *the beloved.* He is saying in other words, "I desire, I pray, I wish, above *all things* . . ." You should underline the words *all things* in your Bible, because this has priority in the mind of John the apostle. Evidently, it is the same way with the Spirit of God. The Bible tells us that "All scripture is given by inspiration of God . . ." (II Timothy 3:16). John, inspired by the Holy Spirit, recorded that we should all prosper and be in good health as our own soul prospers. It is His desire, and it is above *all things* as far as the Spirit of God is concerned. If this letter was written to *one Christian*, then it was written to *all Christians*.

Somebody said, "Jerry, the greatest thing that God would have us to do is get saved."

That's right, but redemption paid for more than your just getting saved and escaping hell. Salvation is a great thing. Of course, it should be the first and foremost step that you take. But don't get the idea that being saved is more important than healing for your body; that being saved is more important than your prospering financially and materially. Jesus of Nazareth paid the price, once and for all, for the sin in your life, for the poverty in your life, and for the sickness in your life with the same substitutionary sacrifice. It is no more important in the eyes of God that you be saved than that you prosper.

Verse 2 reveals to us that in the mind of God above everything else, He wants us to prosper and be in good health even as our soul prospers. I would like to point out that God wants people saved, and He wants them healed just as much as He wants them saved. If He did not, then Jesus would only have paid the price for sin. There would have been some other kind of sacrifice, perhaps a lesser sacrifice for healing.

If you have any idea or opinion that God wants you saved, but you don't know whether or not He wants you healed, then you have missed it. If you say, "I know that God wants me saved, but I don't know if he wants me blessed financially," you have missed the whole point of Calvary.

Calvary has much more involved in it than just delivering you from hell. It is important to God that you are blessed physically and financially, as well as spiritually. God doesn't break these things up into different categories as people do.

Again, of course, it is important to go to heaven. But as far as God is concerned, the sacrifice at Calvary paid the price for your not only escaping hell and having heaven as your eternal destiny, but also while you are in this earth you can live free from sin, grief, sorrow, pain, and the curse of poverty. In the eyes of God there is not any one part of that substitutionary sacrifice any greater than any other part of it. Jesus paid the price in full. Praise God! Salvation, health, and financial prosperity have been made available to you and to me.

Heaven gave its best, Jesus of Nazareth. He paid the price. He died for my sin; He became sick with my sickness, and He became poor that I might become rich.

Yes, I desired to be delivered from hell. I was delivered, and I am not going to hell. Somebody says, "Well, how do you know?" Because the Bible tells me so! "Where?" John 3:16 says, "For God so loved the world, that he gave his only begotten Son, that whosoever believeth in him should not perish, but have everlasting life." Well, if *I can depend on John 3:16,* then bless God, *I can depend on 3 John 2.* Because the same Holy Ghost inspired both Scripture verses.

LET'S MAJOR ON WHAT GOD MAJORS ON

He said that He desires above *all things* that the beloved prosper and be in health even as their soul prospers. I not only have God's Word for it, but I have enjoyed many experiences to prove that it is His will. Notice: the same John who wrote 3 John 2 also wrote the gospel of John. If John was in error in 3 John 2, then it is likely that he missed it in John 3:16. But he didn't miss it. He received his information from God through the inspiration of the Holy Ghost.

"But," some might say, "I had rather get people saved than get them healed."

Listen! There are just as many people in the earth today who are sick physically, as there are spiritually sick. There are just as many people in the earth today who are sick financially as there are spiritually sick. And the substitutionary sacrifice of Jesus, covered it all.

The reason, most of the time, that we have majored on being saved from sin is because in the past, so few dared to preach on healing. Few dared to preach on financial prosperity. God is just as interested in healing sick bodies as He is in saving people from the damnation of hell. God is looking for some men who will not compromise the message of healing — men who will dare believe God and preach His whole message, according to the Word of God.

It is time that Christians — "the beloved" — become concerned and quit dwelling in a realm where we think that one thing is more important than the other, because Jesus Christ of Nazareth paid the same price for it all.

If salvation is available to me, I want it.

If healing is available to me, I want it.

If financial prosperity is available to me, I want it too, praise God!

3

Become Established In The Word

I learned how to be born again through the Word of God. I learned how to get healed through the Word, and I learned how to be prosperous through the Word. It is all in there, and we need to spend much time in the Word. Let's take another look at 3 John 2,4, "Beloved, I wish (I desire, I pray), *above all things* that thou mayest prosper and be in health, even as thy soul prospereth. I have no greater joy than to hear that my children walk in truth."

How can we walk in truth? Jesus prayed, "Sanctify them through thy truth: thy Word is truth" (John 17:17). He is saying that when believers are walking in truth — walking in the Word, they will prosper. You cannot help but prosper when you walk in truth. When you are walking in the Word of God, you are walking in truth, and prosperity comes from walking in truth.

GOD GIVES CHRISTIANS POWER TO GET WEALTH

God said in Deuteronomy 8:18, "But thou shalt remember the Lord thy God: for it is he that giveth thee power to get wealth, that he may establish his covenant which he sware unto thy fathers, as it is this day." God gives Christians power to get wealth, that He may establish His covenant (Word) in the earth. One of the distinguishing marks of a believer, in the sight of God, is prosperity. He said that this is the method that He uses to get His Word established in the earth.

How many people have you known or seen, who were impressed by Christians who said, "It is God's will that Christians be poor". Does that impress you? It did not impress me.

Paul tells us in Romans 11:11, 12 that the reason that God turned to the Gentiles with the gospel was to provoke the Jew to jealousy for the gospel. How many Jews have you ever made jealous for the gospel by telling them that if they become Christians they have to be poor? The descendants of Abraham will not go for poverty, because the old covenant promised them blessings coming in, and blessings going out, blessings in the city, and blessings in the field. You will find that a Jew who is on the old covenant is a prosperous Jew. And you're not going to impress a prosperous Jew who is living according to the old covenant by telling him to live by the new covenant, and then tell him that he has to be poor. That won't make a Jew jealous, and neither will it impress him.

CHRISTIANS HAVE BEEN CALLED "CRUMBS" BECAUSE OF TRADITION

We need to realize that as far as the world is concerned, Christians, in the past, were "crumbs." They were the "scum of the earth." They were the "little people." But I want you to know that the Body of Christ isn't poor any more! Because God is having men preach *prosperity*.

Do you know why men are getting saved at a more rapid rate than natural childbirth today? Because men are preaching *salvation*.

Do you know why people are getting healed, and being delivered from their diseases at a greater rate than ever since the history of the church? Because men are preaching *healing*.

Do you know why the Body of Christ is prospering? Because the Word is being preached concerning *prosperity*. God confirms His Word that is spoken with signs following.

No wonder the Body of Christ stayed so poor all of those years. Most men were preaching that God loves poverty. They thought that if you ever acquired any money, or a better automobile, you were probably sinning. That was the old traditional idea of what God thought about anybody getting blessed.

A man I once met got so angry at me because God was blessing me. You see, he had been a Christian for a long time and he was having a hard time. It seemed as though nothing ever worked for him. The reason was that he didn't know his contract with God. He didn't know what I'm sharing with you. The Bible says that I have a better covenant, founded on better promises; I was just standing on my covenant.

If the Jew can be blessed financially on the old covenant, how much more can a Gentile on the new?

Well, I was just standing on my covenant, praise God; believing what God said. And God was honoring it. He is faithful who has promised. He was confirming His Word.

When God blessed me with a better automobile, *that man became mad.* He was convinced that I was sinning. "Preachers shouldn't have an automobile like that!" he would say. Then when I gave the automobile away, that blew his mind. "Preachers don't give things away," he said. "They are always looking for something."

I ask you: where in the world do you suppose he got an idea like that? From the ministry. That is the image that the ministry has projected to the Body of Christ and the world. That is the reason that half of the members of the Body of Christ didn't want to live by faith. The ministers have projected the *faith life* as a *poor life;* a "barely making it life"; a life that you never know what God is going to do, and you never know, from one moment to the next how things are going to turn out. No wonder that half of the Body of Christ says, "Dear God, I hope that I never have to live by faith."

WE NEED TO "UNLEARN" SOME TRADITIONAL TEACHING

We have been taught wrong. One of the hardest things that the Body of Christ is involved in today is having to *unlearn* those old traditional, wrong ideas that have been rooted in us for so many years. It is not the easiest thing to do, but thank God, that is exactly what the Bible is for. The Bible is called "a two-edged sword". One side of that sword is for the devil and the other side is for you — to clean you up.

Sometimes when you stick that *Sword* in you, it hurts. It doesn't feel too good when you run that *Sword* through yourself and say, "Wait a minute! This is what the Word really says regardless of what I have been taught." Your old traditions will start rising up on the inside of you and say, "Yes, but we were taught it like this fifteen years ago." That *Sword* begins to cut away the things that choke the Word. It hurts, but the best thing for you to do is cut it out. Let God heal the sore, and go on and get established in the Word, and walk in the Word.

John said, "I have no greater joy than to see my children walk in truth." If you walk in truth you are going to prosper. You will remember that He also told us, "Beloved, follow not that which is evil, but that which is good. He that doeth good is of God: but he that doeth evil hath not seen God". I want to point out again that this is not a novice talking. This is an apostle. The same John that told us, "I wish above all things that you might prosper . . .", also said, "Do not follow anything that is evil." Therefore, you can conclude that prosperity is not evil.

Jesus said, "Father, thy will be done on earth as it is in heaven." Is there any poverty in heaven? Then why should I have to live in poverty to serve God? Is there any debt in heaven? Then why should I have to live in debt to serve God? Have you ever visited the throne of God, in prayer, and asked Him to meet a particular need, and He told you, *"I would love to do this for you. Oh, I'd love to meet your need, but you know we have a depression going on up here. I had to lay Jesus off this morning. The angels are on strike, and I had to sell the pearly gate to pay the note on the throne room!"* No! You won't hear that, because they don't have depressions in heaven. They don't have inflation in heaven. They don't drive '49 Fords in heaven. And if they don't drive '49 Fords in heaven, then why should I have to drive one here on earth?

Become established! Walk in the Word and you will be walking in truth, and the truth will set you free.

4

The Root Of All Evil

Invariably, if one starts preaching on *prosperity* someone will say, "But, don't you know that the Bible says that money is the *root of* all evil?"

That is what we have been taught through the years. And that is one of the things that Christians need to *unlearn.* The Bible doesn't say that money is the *root of all evil.* If it did, then God would be guilty of sin. You talk about someone who lives well! Jesus didn't say, *"In my Father's house are many cabins, shacks, and bungalows . . ."* He said, *". . . there are many mansions."* Poor people do not live in mansions. They don't have streets of gold. And they don't have a gate out at the front, carved out of a pearl.

That erroneous teaching is one of the ways that satan uses to deceive Christians concerning prosperity. He would love to stop it. If the truth is not taught, it cannot be confirmed. Jesus tells us that any time one begins to teach revelation knowledge, satan will come immediately to take it away.

A lot of people will get angry and say, "Bless God, that preacher should not be talking about prosperity. He should be talking to people about getting saved." Prosperity is a part of the Gospel, "the good news," and it should be preached.

GOD'S NATURE IS ABUNDANCE
Many people have the idea that the nature of God is miraculous. God's nature is not to perform miracles.

God's nature is abundance; miracles only occur when there is lack.

Somebody said, "Yes, but don't you know, the apostle Paul said, "I have learned to be content?"

Yes, I know, but do you know God's definition of the word *content?* It's found in 2 Corinthians 9:8: "And God is able to make all grace abound towards you, so that you have all sufficiency in all things." I believe that I could be content living like that — couldn't you?

Paul said, "I have learned the secret of facing every situation. I know how to be full. I know how to be abased, and I know how to abound for I have learned the secret. When I am weak, then I am strong". He said, "I can do all things through Christ who strengthens me." *The Amplified version of the Bible* puts it this way: "I can do all things through Christ who infuses inner strength into me." Paul's dependency was on Christ, and all that Christ had done. He is telling us that He was dependent upon all Christ had done through His sacrifice at Calvary.

Let's look at what Paul said about love of money. "For the love of money is the root of all evil: which while some coveted after, they have erred from the faith, and pierced themselves through with many sorrows. But thou, O man of God, flee these things . . ." (I Timothy 6:10, 11).

Some will say, "Ah! See now, there, he says flee those things! And right there, he is talking about money."

That is not what he is saying. He didn't tell you to turn your back on prosperity or financial blessings. He is not saying, "Don't ever have any money." He is talking about fleeing evil: fleeing the love of money, fleeing error, and fleeing covetousness. He is telling us to avoid getting involved with evil because it will cause us to be pierced with many sorrows. It will cause us to be in error. He said, "Charge them that are rich in this world, that they be not highminded, nor trust in uncertain riches, but in the living God, who giveth us richly *all things to enjoy*" (v. 17). Money is a part of *all things*. In other words, don't put your faith in your money because there are many things that your money cannot buy. But put your faith in the living God who gives us richly all things to enjoy.

You have known people who have kept piling up their money *for a rainy day*. They had so much confidence in their money, they would say, "We'll save our money, because one of these days down the road, there may come *a rainy day.*" They programmed themselves to believe that to the point that it never failed, and just about the time retirement came, *so did the rainy day*. And it took every dime they had. They were trusting in uncertain riches.

Don't misunderstand: God is not telling us, and I am not telling you that you shouldn't have a bank account. But I am saying if your faith, and your trust is in your bank account — watch it! Because there are many things that your bank account cannot buy. Put your trust in God. He gives you all things to enjoy.

A gentleman once came to our congregation, who was dying of five major diseases. And any one of them was enough to kill him. We had never seen the man until he came into our service. He was a Minister. He had been in the ministry some 30-35 years. One morning, I was praying and asking the Lord what He wanted me to preach to that group of people. He said, "I want you to preach on healing."

I said, "Why do You want me to preach on healing? Everybody in this congregation is healed."

He said, "Preach on healing." I said, "But Lord, why do You want me to preach on healing? There isn't anybody sick in our congregation."

He said again, "I want you to preach on healing." I said, "All right, I'll preach on healing." I began to meditate the Word. I asked the Lord how He wanted me to approach it; what He wanted me to tell them.

When I got to the service, a woman come in and brought her husband. That man was very ill and bowed over. If you have ever seen someone in the hospital who was dying, this man looked like that. He looked like *death* when they brought him in the door. The wife set him down very gently. He just sat there all shriveled up in that chair. The Spirit of God spoke to me and said, "That is the reason I want you to preach on healing. I want you to *spoon-feed* that man the word of faith, the word of life, the word of health." He said, "I am going to heal him." I preached healing like everybody there needed to hear it.

I could see what was happening on the inside of the man. His faith was rising, and his wife could hardly sit still. When I finished preaching I said, "Bring that man to me." They brought him up, and just as I laid my hands on him the Spirit of God spoke to me.

I began to speak prophetically to the man. "In the Name of Jesus of Nazareth, you will enter in just a few short days, the main thrust of the ministry that God has called you to." As I said before, I didn't know the man, or know that he was a preacher. But I said, "You've been in the ministry, but you have never entered into the main thrust, the main stream of what God has called you to do. But in a few short days you shall enter into the main thrust of what God has called you to do." In the natural, I would not have told a man who looked like he did, anything like that. But it came out of my spirit. If my mind had said it, I wouldn't have said it. When I laid hands on him, there was no physical manifestation that anything happened.

After the service I talked with him. He told me what was wrong with him. One of the diseases that he had was the same disease that killed Aristotle Onasis. And you know as well as I that if money could have bought his healing, he would have been cured. He did not lack in finances. If he had his trust in money, then he found that he had something that money could not buy, the cure. It takes the power of the living God to heal the incurable. When money can't buy health, and medicine can't cure it, then it takes the power of the living God, and that is what we were aiming at.

I started praying and interceding for that man all through the night, groaning and travailing in the spirit for him. The next morning the Spirit of God said to me, "I want you to go over to his home and minister to him. I want you to keep feeding him the Word. I want you to take him some money. He has spent everything he had on doctor bills and pills, and I want you to help him."

I went to the man's home and found him lying on the couch. He was the most pitiful thing that I had ever seen. I said to him, "God sent me here, and I am going to preach the word of health to you, and when you get it in you, then you are going to preach it to me. I'm in this with you, Brother, in the Name of Jesus." I started preaching the Word to him.

One of the diseases, he had, caused him to lose his ability to see clearly. It was impossible for him to read his Bible. His bones had become so deteriorated that every time he rolled over, or turned, he crushed them. His body was so frail. All he could do was sit, and he couldn't do that very long at a time. I ministered to him financially, and I could see God's Word working on the inside of him.

The next day, I had to go to California to conduct a seminar. While I was there, my wife called, just before the service began and said, "They have just rushed Brother Rutledge to the emergency room, and his wife said that the Doctor told her that he would die, and they want you to pray."

Well, when I got to my service, I had all the people stand. We started praising God, worshiping the Lord, and thanking Him for what He had already done. I knew that God would not have me tell that man those things, and then not allow them to come to pass. I was not a false prophet. I have more confidence in my ability to hear the voice of the Good Shepherd. I refuse to hear the voice of a stranger. I believe that I can have what I say. And I knew, that I knew, that I knew, how that was going to turn out! There was no reason for me to go around crying, bawling, and squalling, and begging God to do something. We praised God for how it was going to turn out.

The next Monday morning, when I got back to my office, my secretary called me and told me that someone wanted to see me. She told me that it was the man that we had been ministering to. I said, "Show him in."

In came a fellow who looked like a million dollars! He walked into my office standing tall. Color was back in his flesh. He looked like a brand new man. He pointed his finger at me and said, "Brother! I've got something to tell you."

I said, "I'll bet you do. Sit down and let's hear it." That man had died on the operating table. The doctors stood over him and wrote *deceased* on his records.

He said, "The last thing that I heard was those doctors saying, 'He's dying'." Then everything became dark. I couldn't hear anything else. Then, I knew that I was in the presence of the Lord. The first thing that I said to the Lord was, 'I thought You said I wasn't through.' The Lord didn't say anything to me; He just smiled." The man went on to tell me that He saw his whole life before him. The Lord showed him everything that he had done in the ministry, in the twinkling of an eye. Then the Lord waved His hand and showed him the harvest that is ripe in the world today. Then the man said, "But Lord, I thought you said that I wasn't through. What has all that to do with me? I thought You said that I was just moving into the main thrust of what You called me to do. The Lord still never said a word to me. He just smiled, put His hand on my back and shoved me out into that harvest."

The next thing the man heard was the doctor screaming, "He's alive! He's alive! He's alive!"

That man, at the time of this writing, has preached over seventy-five crusades across the United States. I'll tell you, in the Name of the Lord Jesus, he is one of the most beautiful sights I have ever seen. That's Prosperity!

In these last days, it is being preached more and more that it is God's desire that the Body of Christ prosper; physically, spiritually, financially, and materially. The Body of Christ is going to finance the greatest revival that has ever been experienced on the face of the earth. It is the Body of Christ who is going to funnel the money into it. It is God's will for us to have money as revealed in verse 2 of 3 John, "Beloved, I wish (desire) above all things that thou prosper and be in health even as thy soul prospers."

Somebody says, "But that is talking about spiritual prosperity." Well if it is, the Bible says that all things that were made were made by Him and for Him — a Spirit Being created all matter. Financial blessings come, first of all, in the spirit, then it is manifested in the physical. Let me say it this way: Money begins, first of all, in the spirit because you are involved in a spiritual application when you pray and ask God for finances. Somewhere down the line it will be manifested in the physical. You can't purchase an item with something that you can't see, hold, or feel. Money is a medium of exchange. It takes two people to make a financial transaction. One has the goods and the other has the money to purchase the goods. You don't walk into a store and say, "Listen, I just prayed and asked God for five dollars; I want you to take my prayer as a down payment on what I need." That merchant is interested in trading his goods for something that he can see; particularly if it is *colored green* and has the picture of a famous President printed on it!

Financial prosperity starts out in the spiritual realm, but it will be manifested in the physical realm.

Paul said in Ephesians 1:3, ". . . our Lord Jesus Christ who hath blessed us with *all* spiritual blessings . . ." He went on to say, "And hath raised us up together, and made us sit together in heavenly places in Christ Jesus" (2:6). Peter said, "According as his divine power hath given unto us *all things* that pertain to life and godliness" (2 Peter 1:3) God has, through His divine plan obtained for us ALL THINGS that pertain to life. And the Word says that God has already given them to us. How? Through the substitution sacrifice at Calvary. Jesus paid for it all at Calvary.

If Prosperity is bought and paid for, I want it; it belongs to me. How about you?

Somebody said, "Oh, but you will get all of that when you get to heaven."

I won't need any money when I get to heaven. I won't need an automobile when I get to heaven. I won't need a house when I get to heaven. I need those things now, while I am here on earth.

WE NEED TO HAVE OUR MINDS RENEWED WHERE PROSPERITY IS CONCERNED

Prosperity does not deal with finances only. He said, "I would that you prosper and be in health . . ." He not only wants us to prosper spiritually, but financially, materially, and physically as well. The man I was referring to experienced physical prosperity, something that his money could not buy. If he had been trusting in his money, he would have lost every dime he had, trying to get healed. He would have found out that his money couldn't buy everything that he needed. But, thank God, I want you to know that when he began to prosper in his soul, his mind began to be renewed to God's system and his mind began to think like God thinks — according to the Word. His soul was prospering, Praise God. Therefore, he prospered physically.

The apostle John is not only telling us that God desires above everything else that we prosper spiritually, but financially, materially, and physically, as well.

Someone said, "Well, if He wants all that for me, why doesn't He just do it?"

Because every promise of God is conditional. They do not come on you like ripe apples off a tree. Salvation is available to everyone, even the sinner. If that were not true, you and I would have never been saved. Healing is available to all. Righteousness is available to everyone the

Bible says. Prosperity is available to all, but it does not come on you just because you are a Christian. It is conditional. And the condition is: "I would that you prosper and be in health EVEN AS thy soul prospers."

A MAJOR AVENUE THAT SATAN USES

Christians have either gone from one extreme to the other, where prosperity is concerned. They think that preachers are after their money, or that Christians should be poor. Jesus talked about the deceitfulness of riches in the fourth chapter of Mark. He said that the deceitfulness of riches is one of the major avenues that satan uses trying to make believers non-productive. Satan uses this avenue to try to steal the Word out of a man's heart. Let's find out from God's Word how to avoid this trap. Then let's get all this carnal, traditional knowledge out of our thinking. The Word does not say that Christians are supposed to be poor. God does not love poverty. You may find that you will have to start over, and put everything that you have *heard* about what God *thinks* about prosperity, upon the shelf. Get into the Word. Read the Word, and meditate the Word. Then you will find that you will not pick those religious ideas up from that shelf again. As you continue in the Word, you will know the TRUTH and the truth will set you free.

5

A Closer Look At Man

The Spirit of God once said to me, "Son, you are going to prosper materially, financially, and physically in direct proportion to the Prosperity of your Soul." He said, "Son, I said, 'even as thy soul prospers'."

If your soul is not prospering then you are not going to prosper materially. If your soul is not prospering, you are not going to prosper financially.

You may say, "Well, what about the rich sinner?" Well, what about him! That person has only a *temporary prosperity*. It will not last. I don't care how many of those beer drinking, whiskey guzzling, people you know who are doing whatever they want to do, with no regard for God yet seem to be prosperous, it is only temporary. The Bible says, ". . . the wealth of the sinner is laid up for the just" (Proverbs 13:22). I like the way the Amplified *Version of the Bible says this same verse of Scripture:* "A good man leaves an inheritance (of moral stability and goodness) to his children's children, and the wealth of the sinner (finds its way eventually) into the hands of the righteous, for whom it was laid up." I am that righteous person; aren't you? It will eventually come into the righteous' hands. It belongs to us, praise God!

A TEMPORARY RESERVOIR

The sinner who possesses wealth is only a *temporary reservoir*. Satan finds somebody on whom he can dump those finances on; because he wants to keep them out of the hands of the Body of Christ. He knows that if the Body of Christ ever gets their hands on those finances, they will put it into the gospel. And once it is put into the gospel, God's power is manifested. When God's power is manifested, people are healed, they are saved, they are delivered, and they are set free. As God's power is manifested, the Body of Christ begins to mature. All the spots, the blemishes, and the wrinkles begin to disappear. The perfecting of the Saints is what ushers in the soon appearing of the Lord Jesus Christ. I believe that point of *"eventually"* has come. You can get in on it now if you wish, or you can wait until you get to Heaven. I want mine now! Praise God! I need it now. I have a lot of gospel to preach, and it takes more money to preach it now than it ever has before.

Christians will prosper physically, financially, and materially in direct proportion to the prosperity of their souls.

MAN ? A TRIUNE BEING

You may have this question in your thinking: "What do you mean when you say that I will prosper in direct proportion to the prosperity of my soul?"

Well, you need to get this fact established right now. *Man is triune in his being.* Man is a spirit, he has a soul, and he lives in a body.

You are not a soul: *you have a soul.*

You are not a body: *you live in a body.*

You do not have a spirit: *you are a spirit.*

You do not have a human: you are a human.

You are a *spirit*, you have a *soul*, and you live in a *body*.

The fleshly body that you can see is *your "earth suit."* Remember Paul told us, ". . . to be absent from the body is to be present with the Lord." If you are not reborn — recreated, while you are here on the earth, you will be present with another *lord, satan.* Spirit beings do not dwell in the earth without bodies. So, in order for you to live in this earth, you — a *spirit,* must have an *"earth suit",* and this is the purpose for the flesh or physical body.

Paul says, "And the very God of peace sanctify you wholly (not holy, but *wholly*); and your whole *spirit* and *soul* and *body* be preserved blameless unto the coming of our Lord Jesus Christ" (I Thessalonians 5:23). This shows that man is three parts. Hebrews 4:12 tells us that the Word of God has the ability to discern the spirit, the soul, and the body. This tells us that man is a spirit, he has a soul, and he lives in a body.

By now, you know that John said by the inspiration of the Holy Spirit, in 3 John 2, that God desires that you prosper and be in health as your soul prospers. Notice: EVEN AS YOUR SOUL PROSPERS.

You may say, "Well, if all of that is true, then what is my soul?"

If you will study the Word of God, you will find that *the soul* of man is made up of his mind, his will, his emotions; his thinking faculties.

You may say, "Well, what about where the Bible says that if a man doesn't accept Jesus he loses his soul?"

This is exactly right. When a person dies and goes to hell without accepting Jesus as Lord of his life, he has no control over his soul. He ends up in a place that was created for satan and his angels. He has an everlasting sense of falling, because hell is described as the bottomless pit. Can you imagine what that must be like? To have no control over your thinking faculties, and feeling like you are *falling constantly* — for eternity?

I once fell off the top of a house, and I thought I would never hit bottom. I cannot imagine going through eternity always feeling as though I am falling. That would be a terrible state of mind.

Your next question may be, "If my soul is made up of my mind, my will, my emotions, and my thinking faculties, and I am going to prosper in direct proportion to the prosperity of my soul, then, how do I cause my soul to prosper? What constitutes a prosperous soul?"

A prosperous soul is one in which the mind is renewed, the will conformed, the emotions controlled, and the thinking faculties selective of that which it thinks. Remember this: A prosperous soul is one in which the mind is renewed, converted, revived, and healed by the Word of God. The word convert means to turn around. Romans 12:1, 2 tells us: "I beseech you therefore brethren, by the mercies of God, that ye present your bodies a living sacrifice, holy, acceptable unto God, and be not conformed to this world: but be ye transformed by the renewing of your mind."

LET'S FIND OUT HOW THE SOUL PROSPERS

Number one: *A prosperous soul thinks like God thinks*. If your mind has been renewed to God's way of thinking, it has been renewed to God's system; it has been renewed to the counsel of God; it has been converted.

Before you were saved, your mind was fouled up with the wisdom of this world. You thought as the world thinks. And the world thinks, "Well, if you only have five dollars, don't dare get rid of it because you never know; it may get worse."

The renewed mind thinks, "Give and it shall be given unto you good measure, pressed down, shaken together, and running over shall men give unto your bosom." If you have a prosperous soul, your mind is renewed to God's system.

Number two: *In a prosperous soul the will is conformed.* You may ask, "What do you mean by the will is conformed? Doesn't God want a broken will?"

Now what in the world would God want with a bunch of people who have broken wills? He doesn't want a broken will. That is the reason that Jesus of Nazareth did what He did at Calvary. He wanted man's will to stay intact. God wants your will conformed to His will, not broken.

You may say, "Well, the only way I can get my will conformed to God is to break it."

No, it's not. Jesus said in John 15:7, "If ye abide in me, and my words abide in you, ye shall ask what ye will, and it shall be done unto you." The key to a conformed will is to abide in Christ and have His Word abiding in you. If His Word abides in you, then your will becomes the same as God's will. You will find that you'll never ask anything in prayer out of lust. It will be the perfect will of God when you pray because you think like He thinks. That constitutes a prosperous soul.

Number three: *In a prosperous soul the emotions are controlled.* If your emotions are brought under subjection to the Word of God, you will not be moved by what you see or feel. In order to prosper in God's way of thinking, your five physical senses and your emotions have to be under control. When you ask God to meet a financial need, and it doesn't look like anything is happening, your emotions could run away with you. And you could sit down and want to beat your head against the table and say, "Why isn't it working? I don't understand." When you have no evidence according to your five physical senses that your need is met, your emotions will run away with you. This is the reason a prosperous soul is one in which the emotions are controlled. Your emotions are controlled by the Word of God. When your *sense-gate* called "sight", starts talking to you and says, "Boy! I don't see any change, the problem still exists." That's when the prosperous soul being to take action. *It will feed that sense-gate the Word.* It will say, "In the name of Jesus, I'm not moved by what I see. I am moved by what I believe, and I believe the Word that Jesus said. He said that what things soever I desire when I pray, that I should believe I receive them, and I shall have them. I have prayed, and I know that I know that God is faithful who has promised. He said that He would supply all my need according to His riches in glory by Christ Jesus. I don't care how I feel about it, or what it looks like. The Word says it, and SO BE IT!" Controlled emotions constitutes a prosperous soul.

Number four: *The thinking faculties of a prosperous soul is selective of what it thinks.* Do not sit around and dwell on negative thoughts if you want to have a prosperous soul. That is a *luxury* that Christians cannot afford. You can't dwell on what you see on TV, or what you read in the paper. You cannot dwell on what all the sinners and half the Christians in town are saying. You must be selective in what you think. A prosperous soul thinks on the things that are found in the Word. Think on things that are good, things that are lovely, things that are just, things that are of a good report. Paul said, "Think on these things."

When you are believing God for prosperity, satan will try to lodge a thought in your thinking faculties that will prove to you that it is not going to work. He likes to bring up the experience of somebody else. "You know Brother So and So believed that, and he lost everything he had." You dwell on that and you dwell on it and you dwell on it; the next thing that will develop is *worry*. *Worry is meditation on negative thoughts: the thoughts of satan.* You start worrying about it, and then it is not going to just stay in your head. It will drop down in your heart. And Jesus said that out of the abundance of the heart, the mouth will speak. When it leaves your head and gets down into your heart, you will start talking it. You will talk lack; you'll talk *poverty;* and you'll talk that *it's not working. Then spiritual law is released, and you will have what you say.*

The prosperous soul is one in which the mind is renewed, the will conformed, the emotions controlled, and the thinking faculties are selective. The key to living in the kind of prosperity that God has designed for the Body of Christ is to start thinking right. Talk like He talks. Dwell on what the Word says, and get your emotions under control.

JESUS WAS A MAN WITH A PROSPEROUS SOUL

Somebody said, "Yes, but Jesus didn't even have a place to lay His head He was so poor."

That is ridiculous! The reason that Jesus did not have a place to lay His head was because He was too busy ministering to those that did. Humanity needed Him.

If Jesus was so poor, then what was Judas doing? He was the treasurer. Poor people do not have treasurers. Evidently they must have had something in the treasury because Judas was stealing out of it from time to time, and nobody missed what was being taken except Jesus. If they only had a few quarters here and there, don't you know that the first time James and John looked into the bag, they would have noticed that some money was gone? They would have called *fire* down from heaven?

Poor men do not have twelve men working for them and supporting their families. Jesus did. Then He broadened His Evangelistic Association by commissioning seventy others. How would you like to have seventy on your staff if you were poor? That is something to think about. Jesus had every situation under control, because His mind was renewed to the Abrahamic covenant. His will was conformed to God's will. He said, "Father, not my will but thy will be done . . ." His emotions were under control. Jesus was not moved by what He saw. If He was, He would have run off and hidden when He had to feed five thousand men, plus the women and children, with five loaves and two fishes. Jesus' emotions were under control. He was selective about what He thought. He was a man with a prosperous soul. If you don't know anybody else that lived this way, study the ministry of Jesus again. He prospered in every thing that He set His hand to do.

This same prosperity is available to Christians today. Praise the Lord!

6
True Prosperity

When John wrote, "Beloved, I wish above all things that thou mayest prosper *and* be in health . . . ," he was wishing two different things for us. That word *"and"* is a conjunction, it connects two thoughts. In Texas, when you see the word *and*, that means *he "ain't" through talking yet!* He is desiring two things for the beloved. *"Prosper AND be in health"* are connected. Don't take one without the other. Many times people drop the idea of prosperity.

"Well," somebody says, "What does he mean by 'prosper'? Does that just mean having money?"

Not necessarily. Prosperity, in the eyes of God, is not just having a lot of money. There are many things that money cannot buy, but faith in the Word can get. Prosperity does not include only money. But let's not go to the extreme and exclude money. People will say, "Well, you know that money can't buy everything, and there are a lot of things more important than having all the money you need."

That's right. But on the other hand let's not exclude money, because it is a part of prosperity. The word *barter* means to trade or exchange one commodity or service for another. Money is *a medium of exchange*, and we use it to make transactions or trades. We need money for this purpose. The Bible says in the writings of Peter, that God has obtained for us *all things* that pertain to life and godliness. Money pertains to life and God has obtained *all things* for us.

Somebody said, "If this is so, why don't I have any money then?"

If you haven't guessed by now, that is the reason I am teaching on *Prosperity of the Soul.* The Body of Christ has not walked in the area of financial prosperity because so few dared to teach on it. "If you start talking about money they won't like you," some would say. "After all," they say, "preachers are not supposed to talk about money." That is the reason so few of them ever have any money. They are afraid to talk about it. They have believed that "Money is the root of all evil," instead of the truth which says, *"The love of money* is the root of all evil."

John said, "I would — desire, that you prosper . . ." Money is not the only thing involved in prosperity, but it plays a vital role in it. According to the following Scripture verse, God gets great pleasure when His people are prosperous. "Let them shout for joy, and be glad, that favor my righteous cause: yea, let them say continually, Let the Lord be magnified, which hath pleasure in the prosperity of his servant" (Psalm 35:27).

People have had the mistaken idea that if any member of the Body of Christ ever prospers it is because they have gotten off into sin. If the preacher gets a new automobile, "He isn't humble any more." Satan wants them to believe that, because he realizes that if the Body of Christ ever gets their hands on what rightfully belongs to them, it won't stick to them. They will put it into the gospel, the work of the ministry. They will revive this old world as it has never been revived before.

DON'T HOARD MONEY: KEEP
THE CYCLE GOING

Since the Bible says that the wealth of the sinner has been laid up for the just, and that it will eventually find its way into the hands of the righteous, you should *start walking around with your hands open.* It belongs to you! Praise God! However, I wish to emphasize this: Don't hoard money. It doesn't belong to you for that purpose. Hoarding up all the money you can get because, "You never know what is going to happen tomorrow and you must save for a rainy day," is not a testimony to the Lord.

God wants you to have money and prosperity so you can share it. When you share it, He keeps adding more to you. You start a cycle that is unending. The key to that cycle is consistency. You don't just give once and receive a return, and then get so stuck on the return that you decide that you aren't going to give any more. You must cast your bread upon the water and not many days hence, it shall return unto you. (Read Ecclesiastes 11:1). If you keep casting bread out there, somewhere down the road every wave is going to bring in a return. Consistency keeps the cycle working. *The worst thing you can do when every* wave starts bringing in a return is to turn your back on God, and hoard up all that you can set your hands on.

GOD GIVES POWER TO GET WEALTH

God told Israel in Deuteronomy 8:18 to remember that it is God who gave them the power to get wealth in order that He might establish His covenant. You will find that all the strong men of God in the Old Testament were men of wealth. Abraham was a man of great wealth. Job was the richest man in all of the east.

Somebody said, "Yes, but Job lost everything he had."

Wait a minute! Read the closing chapter of the book of Job. God blessed Job with double of everything he lost. If Job was the richest man in the east and he lost it all, what do you think that made him when God doubled everything that he once had?

I dare say that there has never been a man who has tapped into the resource of wealth that Solomon did. That does not mean that it is not available. God desires it for *the beloved.*

TWO EXTREMES WHERE RICHES ARE CONCERNED

Many people get cross because of this type of teaching. They have the idea that all we are dwelling on is money. No! I am not dwelling on money, but that does not mean that I should exclude the teaching on it. Don't misunderstand. The first time that you allow money to become priority, you are in trouble. You can go from one extreme to the other. Jesus showed us that this is one of the main avenues in which satan will use to steal the Word from the people in whom the Word has been sown. He talks about afflictions, persecutions, the lust of other things, and the cares of this world, and the deceitfulness of riches.

There are two extremes where riches are concerned. People will get their eyes on the riches and put their trust in them, or they will believe that Christians are not supposed to have any riches. They should live in poverty. Both are deceit and deception designed by satan to keep the Christian non-productive. If one extreme says, "Get your eyes on riches and put your trust in them," and the other says, "We are not supposed to have any riches," then evidently there is a truth in the middle that you and I can get on and be blessed by it. I believe that if you will weigh both sides on this issue, you will find that according to Psalm 35:27, God delights in the prosperity of His people.

The key is this:

You should have prosperity: don't let prosperity have you.

You should have money: don't let money have you.

You should have things: don't let things have you.

7
The Principle Of Giving And Receiving

God has blessed me in the short number of years since I accepted Jesus as the Lord of my life. I am not saying that I have huge amounts of money and that I never have to trust God for financial assistance. I am saying that He has blessed my family and me in a tremendous way, and we are living better now than we ever have before.

When God began to prosper me and my family, we began to see that we could not allow *things* to possess us. I would like to share an example of how I learned this.

I had just left Brother Kenneth Copeland's organization, where I was an Associate Minister, and I had been invited to hold a week's meeting in an Assembly of God church in a very small town. It was the very first meeting on my own. We had a total of less than seventy-five people in that meeting. The same group came every night. Many of them were not members of that church. Several of the church members weren't coming.

I had made up my mind that God had called me to preach the gospel, to be instant in season and out, and that those people were not my source. God was my source, and if He could not take care of me, then He should have told me back there in 1969 before I got involved with this. As a result of relying on Him as my source, in that week's meeting, with only seventy-five people, God blessed me with $5,100. I didn't know that there was that much money in the world! I shall never forget it as long as I live. *Fifty-one hundred dollars!*

When I got home, I spent every quarter of it in order to buy office furniture, typewriters, and equipment to be used to spread the gospel. I hired a secretary. It got us started, praise God!

Just twelve days before, I had asked God for $5,000 to start this ministry. In less than two weeks time He blessed me again with some tape duplicating equipment that was worth about $5,000.

When I got home that night after I had set that brand new equipment up in my office, my wife and I rejoiced. It looked as though God was on our side, even though half of the Christians doubted it. But we had the evidence to prove that He was on our side. I was in my study praising the Lord, just fellowshipping with Him and thanking Him, when suddenly I heard this come up in my spirit. I shall never forget it! He said, "Son, I want you to give part of that tape duplicating equipment away."

I thought, "That must have been something I ate! That couldn't be the Lord. I haven't even used it yet." I started doing something else so I wouldn't hear it again. But every time I got quiet I heard it again. I had two sets of duplicating equipment. One of them was worth about $3,600, and the other was worth about $1,500. The Lord was telling me, "I want you to give one part of that duplicating equipment to another minister. He needs it right now."

I said, "Lord! You just gave it to me."

He said, "I know it, but I want you to give it to him."

I said, "But Lord, I haven't even used it yet. Can't I just run down there and make a few tapes on it?"

He said, "No, I want you to give it to him."

I didn't understand that. I thought, "Well! That isn't fair." It was then that the Lord brought something to my remembrance.

I was in a television studio in Dallas one day, preaching on a program there. I wore casual clothes to the studio, intending on changing into my suit before going on the air. When I arrived at the studio, I had all of my clothes *except my tie!* The program was to be aired over thirteen different stations and there I was without a tie. I sat there in the dressing room and said, "Lord, what am I going to do about a tie?" Someone came in and offered me a tie that wouldn't have matched anything that I would have ever worn! I said, "Lord, I believe that you can do better than that! I can't go on that program wearing that *weird looking tie!*"

As I sat there a fellow came in and asked if Jerry Savelle was there. I heard someone say, "Yes, I believe he is in the dressing room."

I was surprised when a friend of mine walked in, and I asked him what he was doing there. He said, "Well, it just beats anything I have ever seen! I was down at this men's clothing store. I had just bought myself a tie. I was about to put it on when God told me to take it over to Channel 11 and give it to you."

I said, "Praise the Lord! I don't doubt it, Brother. Help me get it on."

He said, "I fussed with God all the way over here saying, 'Don't I get to wear it once'? And He said, "No, I wanted you to buy that tie for Jerry."

As I fussed about the equipment that God told me to give away, the Lord reminded me of the tie incident. He said, "Son, I presented that piece of equipment to you, so that I could bless you with greater, by your giving it away. Son, I don't know whether you realize it, but you are a little short of capital right now."

I said, "You know that You are right."

He said, "Would you like some more finances to keep things running smoothly"?

I said, "I certainly would."

He said, "That is the reason why I gave you this piece of equipment. I want you to give it for the gospel's sake, and I will bless you one-hundred times it's value. I'm not trying to take something from you. I don't give you something and then just take it away. I am trying to create an avenue to bless you. I'll provide you with even greater equipment and finances to go with it."

That was when I became really cheerful about giving — quickly! In fact, I was lying on my face before the Lord asking Him to forgive me for acting the way I did. I said, "Father, I want you to know right now, I am committing myself in Jesus' name to give the very shirt off my back for the gospel's sake, if You desire it. I'll never hesitate again when You instruct me to give."

He said, "Son, that is what I have been wanting to hear. You have never truly given until you are ready to give it all." That blessed me! And from that point on, I made up my mind that things would never again possess me.

When God blessed me with my first airplane, I was so glad. I had believed God and stood on the Word for two years for that piece of equipment. Two years, night and day, I confessed, "I believe that I have the perfect airplane for this ministry." Two years later, thank God, it was manifested. I didn't owe a quarter on it. The very first thought that came up on the inside of me the day it was given to me was, "What if God asks me to give it away?" I told Him right there on the scene as I laid my hands on that airplane, and received it into this ministry: "Now God, in the name of Jesus, if You tell me to give it away before dark, I'll do it without hesitation." He allowed me to use that airplane for about a year, then He instructed me to sell it and put some of the money into other ministries. The return on that is still coming in, praise the Lord!

God is interested in the prosperity of His people, but the most dangerous thing that His people can do when God begins to prosper them is to allow those things to possess them.

I had a very close minister friend. I thought very highly of him, and I desired to give money into his ministry. I didn't have a quarter. I said, "Lord, I want to finance that man's ministry. I want to give to him. I want to support his ministry, but I don't have a dime."

The Lord said to me, "Son, my Word says that I not only multiply seed that is sown, but I am also the Provider of the seed." He said, "Use your faith, and I'll provide your seed to sow."

I said, "All right, in the name of Jesus, I believe I receive seed to sow." My wife and I joined hands, and we asked God to bless us with finances not for ourselves, but that we could invest in that man's ministry. In a couple of days, while the man was still in our town ministering in this meeting, God blessed us with some money. The first thing that satan hit me with when I had it in my hands was, "Boy, you could buy groceries this week with that money. You know you have a light bill coming up." I thought of ninety things that I could spend that money on right at that moment. But I didn't ask God to give it to me for my own use. I had asked Him to give it to me to give to someone else. Just at the moment when God blessed me with the money, there was a hesitation. The thought came, "You could do this and you could do that." The same thought came to my wife. But we made up our mind, "NO! In the name of Jesus, this is the avenue God is going to use to bless us, praise God! He has given us this amount of money, and we receive it in the name of Jesus to give to someone else." We invested it into that man's ministry, and God rewarded! We didn't go without groceries, and our light bill was paid, thank God. We had more than enough to do what we had to do that week.

The most dangerous thing that you can get into when God begins to bless you is to allow material things to possess you. Giving is the avenue that God uses to bring greater blessings. This is the reason that John the apostle went on to say, "I desire that you prosper, and be in health even as your soul prospers." He is actually telling us that we will not prosper physically, financially, or materially if our souls are not prospering.

If your soul is experiencing soulish poverty, you are going to experience financial poverty, material poverty, and physical poverty. Even though God delights in the prosperity of His servants, it is conditional. It doesn't come to you automatically. It comes to you in direct proportion to the prosperity of your soul.

8
Walking In Truth

If you have a prosperous soul your mind is renewed to God's Word. Your will is conformed to God's will; your emotions are controlled and brought under subjection to the Word of God; and your thinking faculties are selective of that which you think. You will think according to the instructions found in Philippians 4:8, "Finally, brethren, whatsoever things are true, whatsoever things are honest, whatsoever things are just, whatsoever things are pure, whatsoever things are lovely, whatsoever things are of good report; if there be any virtue, and if there be any praise, think on these things." Then, thank God! Prosperity (physically, financially, and materially) cannot help but come your way. John said that He had no greater joy than to hear that *His children walk in truth.* Jesus said in John 17:17, ". . . thy word is truth." We are talking about the Word of God. Your soul becomes prosperous as you walk in truth. *To walk in truth is to walk in the Word of God.*

We read in Psalm 19, "The law of the Lord is perfect, converting the soul: The testimony of the Lord is sure, making wise the simple" (v. 7). "The *Word* of the Lord is perfect, converting the soul . . ." The word *convert* means to restore, revive, heal, and renew. A simple definition of the word convert means to make an about face, to turn around. In other words, God is telling us that it takes walking in truth, or walking in His Word, to convert one's soul. He is saying, "I will prosper you financially, materially, and physically, as your soul is turned around." When the soul stops thinking on carnal knowledge and magnifying the wisdom of this world, and it is converted (makes an about face and chooses God's way, His wisdom, His counsel, and His thoughts), then prosperity cannot help but come. "The statutes of the Lord are right, rejoicing the heart. The commandment of the Lord is pure, enlightening the eyes (God gives wisdom and understanding). The fear of the Lord is clean, enduring for ever: the judgments of the Lord are true and righteous altogether (His judgments, His Word is true and righteous altogether!)" (vv. 8,9).

God has no greater joy than that we walk in His Word — His truth. When I do this, my soul prospers.

Another Scripture passage that bears out this truth is Psalms 1:1-3. "Blessed is the man that walketh not in the counsel of the ungodly, nor standeth in the way of sinners, nor sitteth in the seat of the scornful. But his delight is in the law (Word), of the Lord; and in his law (Word) doth he meditate day and night. And he shall be like a tree planted by the rivers of water, that bringeth forth his fruit in his season; his leaf also shall not wither; and whatsoever he doeth shall prosper." He prospers because he delights in the Word. He meditates the Word. In other words, he is walking in truth. I like the way God uses words like *whatsoever, everything,* and *all.* It sounds to me as if there are no exceptions. I like the way the *Amplified Version of the Bible* translates this same passage: ". . . everything he does shall come to full maturity."

"Beloved, follow not that which is evil but that which is good. He that doeth good is of God: but he that doeth evil hath not seen God" (3 John 11). Well! We have found that a prosperous soul comes by *walking in truth — walking in God's Word,* and the above verse tells us that a prosperous soul comes from *following not that which is evil,* but *that which is good.* We now need a definition of *what is good,* and *where the good comes from* that we should follow after. James 1:17 tells us: Every good gift (*not most of them, or some of them, but EVERY one of them*], and every perfect gift is from above, and cometh down from the Father of light, with whom there is no variableness, neither shadow of turning." If the Apostle John said, "Follow that which is good:" and if God is the author of good and perfect gifts, then He is telling us to follow after that of which God is the Author.

God is not the Author of most of those silly television commercials, like, "There is a big headache out there waiting for you." If you follow that advice, you will not have a prosperous soul. Neither is God the Author of, "When you can't suppress a cough, let Vicks do it for you." I am not preaching against medicine. I am talking about converting our souls: thinking like God thinks. I have never approached the throne of God and found that Jesus had to take off a few days because He had the *flu,* and God had Him on *Vicks.*

Jesus has no use for Vicks and Jerry doesn't either. If I didn't know what I know about God's Word, *Vicks* would be a very close friend of mine. If I didn't know what I know about the Word of God, Bufferin would be a very close friend of mine. I am saying, that before my soul was converted, my mind renewed, my will conformed to the Will of God, my emotions controlled, and my thinking faculties selective, *Vicks, Bufferin,* and *Anacin,* were friends of mine. Why? Because I was sick, I needed something to relieve the pain, and I didn't know that God's Word was health to my flesh.

The moment my soul was converted, I didn't need those medicines any longer because I began to prosper physically. It is up to each Christian to do something with

their soul. It must be converted through the Word of God
— by walking in truth.

The problem with a lot of Christians today is that
they are reborn but they are still living by carnal
knowledge. They haven't done anything about prospering
their souls. They have escaped hell, but they still live like
carnal men while they are on the earth.

Your soul wasn't recreated when you accepted Jesus
as Lord of your life. The real you, the spirit man on the
inside of your body, was recreated in the image and
likeness of God. Jesus saved you through His
substitutionary sacrifice at Calvary. But it is up to you to
convert your soul. God doesn't just snap His finger and all
of a sudden you stop thinking bad thoughts. Converting
your soul comes through meditating the Word. God gave
us His Word. He gave you a copy of His Word, and He
sent the Teacher of His Word, the Holy Spirit, to help you
get your soul converted. John said, "Follow that which is
good."

Acts 10:38 says, "How God anointed Jesus of
Nazareth with the Holy Ghost and with power: who went
about doing good, and healing all that were oppressed of
the devil; for God was with him." *Jesus went about
healing, and God considered what He did was good.* He
was healing all that were oppressed of the devil. If healing
is not good in the sight of God, than Jesus should not have
healed anyone. But if healing is *good,* then God is the
Author of it. His Word says that every good gift and
every perfect gift comes from God, in whom there is no
variableness.

It is not pleasing to God for someone to say, "Healing
is not for us today," or "Well, you never know whether or
not it is God's will to heal." The Bible plainly tells you that
God is the Author of every good thing and that Jesus

went about doing good. Jesus went about healing the sick and oppressed.

John said, "Follow that which is good." If you think that healing is from the devil, and it is not a gift of God, then you are going to miss out on physical prosperity.

Prosperity of the soul comes when one walks in truth, and follows that which is good. When one follows that which is good, his soul begins to prosper.

You cannot prosper in the soulish realm without the aid of God's Word. You must walk in truth: walk in the counsel of God.

9
Walking In Truth Is Your Responsibility

If you do not know what God's Word says about physical prosperity, you will never experience it. In other words, before you can prosper physically you must prosper in your soul. Your soul which is made up of your mind, your will, your emotions, and your thinking faculties, has to be converted. Jesus paid the price to save or recreate your spirit. Your spirit was recreated at the time you accepted the new birth. But nothing necessarily happened to your soul.

The responsibility of converting your soul is yours. God gave you the tools that it takes to convert your soul: His Word and His Spirit. But unless you take advantage of the tools that He gives you, you will go through life with a soul that is not prosperous. You will be saved, but you will still think *carnally:* the same way you thought before you were saved. You may not be quite as ugly, or think all the same ugly thoughts that you did before you were saved. But listen! It is just as carnal for a Christian to go around thinking that it is not the will of God to heal as it is for a Christian to go around cusing. Both are wisdom that comes from satan: sensual, devilish, earthy, and carnal. Any person who reads the Bible ought to have sense enough to figure out that it is God's will to heal.

You may say, "Well, He didn't heal me. And He didn't heal *Brother So and So.*"

I am sorry, but I refuse to take that as evidence. I cannot allow *Brother So and So* to be the basis upon which I believe God. I'll just keep on believing Brother Jesus!

Jesus believed this, and He is doing well! He bore my sickness and my disease at Calvary. But He isn't sick any more! He got healed. The Bible says that He bore it all — praise God! He took upon Himself the sickness and disease of this world. And the Bible says that His visage was so marred that it didn't even resemble the shape of a human being. You cannot conceive in your mind what a body would look like that has been stricken with every disease that is known to mankind. But Jesus of Nazareth bore it all. That is the reason that Roman soldier stood back and said, "My God! This has to be the Son of God." No one but Jesus could have done that and still be able to say with a loud voice, "It is finished!"

But thank God! I want you to know that Jesus doesn't have any of those diseases any more. The visage of Jesus isn't marred any more. He doesn't have any problem with His throat or with His back. He is not in pain in His legs any more. Jesus is not in the agony that He suffered at Calvary. In fact, the Bible teaches that when the voice of the Son of God is heard, it is like the voice of many waters. Does that sound like someone with a sore throat? Jesus is healed and doing well, seated at the right hand of God. And thank God! I John 4:17 tells us that as *He is so are we.*

My throat is well, too, because Jesus bore my sore throat. If He bore that sore throat, there is no need of me bearing it now!

I didn't learn to think like this by reading *Mad Magazines*, and certainly not *True Confessions!* They aren't true! The Word of God is THE TRUE CONFESSION! And it takes the Word of God to convert one's soul.

THE MIND IS THE BATTLEGROUND

When a problem arises does your mind scream out, "Oh, Dear God! What am I going to do?" If it does, you need to have your soul converted. When you have your soul converted and you begin to walk in truth following that which is good, when a problem arises, the Word of God will rise up out of your heart (spirit) and your mind will be in agreement with your heart. They are fellowshipping together. Instead of your spirit crying out one thing and your head screaming something else, they will both say, "In the name of Jesus! It is written . . ." They will both be talking the Word.

The biggest warfare that one can have, and especially a Christian, is the warfare in his head. The biggest battles of satan are fought in the mind. *The mind is the battleground.* What do you suppose it would be like if you could get your mind to cooperate with your spirit and the Word of God? That would be *peace*. Peace! Hallelujah! The only way that you will get your mind quiet, and to think like God, is by walking in truth and following that which is good. You may say, "But Jerry, are you telling me that you never have any bad thoughts?"

That is not what I am saying. But I'll tell you this, the moment bad thoughts come to my mind, I do not have to tolerate them and neither do you! You can think on good things just as quickly as the devil can put a bad thought in there. I refuse to sit around and think in terms of lack. I refuse to think in terms of poverty. I refuse to think in terms of failure. Oh yes, the thought comes every once in a while. I have many opportunities to fail, but I refuse to entertain it. Because if I entertain that thought, I will begin to dwell on it. If I dwell on it, that will cause worry, and once it begins to be in the *form of worry*, it will leave my head and drop down into my spirit. The next thing I know, I will be talking it. Once I start talking it, I will have what I say.

No wonder the devil attacks the mind first. He wants to put bad thoughts in there. For instance, "You're not going to get your healing this time," and "Why, God can't supply that much money to you by Friday night!" If you sit there and dwell on those thoughts, satan will paint you the most beautiful picture of failure that you have ever seen. Satan will paint you a picture of failure and defeat if you will allow him to do so.

SHOVE BAD THOUGHTS OUT OF YOUR MIND

You can pick up your newspaper and read all the bad news, watch three hours of television, then go talk to your neighbor before you go to bed, and I will guarantee that you will have the opportunity, before the night is over, to think and dwell on thoughts of defeat, failure, sickness, lack, depression, and hard times. If you entertain those thoughts, satan will paint you a beautiful picture of all this. It will affect you right now.

The Word of God is designed to help us fight the battle. If you will allow the Word of God to be the thoughts in your mind, entertain those thoughts, and dwell on the Word of God, you will say, "My God shall supply all my need according to His riches in glory by Christ Jesus! That's my God! That is my God who shall supply all my needs . . ." You can't think in terms of lack when you speak and dwell on the Word of God. I challenge you to spend thirty minutes dwelling on the Word and speaking it, and see if you can think thoughts of failure. You cannot. You can shove negative thoughts from your mind by replacing them with the thoughts of God and speaking the Word.

IT TAKES MORE THAN JUST READING THE WORD OF GOD

The reason a lot of people have a problem converting their souls is because they thought that it comes by only reading the Word of God. Much more is involved than that. Yes, you must *read the Word*, but if that is all you do, you will never get there. There comes a time when you have to *meditate the Word*. That means to dwell on it. *Fix your mind on the Word.* Say it to yourself. Allow the Spirit of God to reveal to you what He is saying. Many Christians read the Word of God hundreds of times, but they still cannot tell you a word that it says. I am talking about *revelation knowledge*. They may be able to quote several chapters, but that does not mean that they are operating in revelation knowledge.

The Word of God is lifeless until it lodges down in your heart (spirit), and you allow it to work in your life. Many unsaved people read the Bible, but it doesn't mean anything to them, even though it is the Holy Bible, the Word of God. But, if they will sit there and dwell on what the Word says (think about it), and allow God to plant that seed in their heart, then it will become alive to them and they will act on it. That is how you were saved. You didn't just read the Bible. It began to mean something to you as you dwelt on what the Word was saying. You realized, "Hey! I can apply that to myself right now!"

Get that Word in your heart; dwell on it; meditate it; fix your mind on the Word and think about it. Then, the moment you wake up in the morning, your feet will hit the floor and you will start confessing God's Word. If you have only five minutes to read a Scripture passage, do it. You may not be able to read the Word all day, but you can dwell on what you read that morning. You can run it over and over, and meditate what the Word says.

My family knows that I spend a lot of time meditating the Word of God. This is what set me free; there is no sense in quitting now. Many times we will be driving down the road, on our way to a service and my children won't be talking much. They know that I am getting ready to preach, and that I am running over in my consciousness what I have just read. Many times my family and I have driven on the highway for hours, and all of a sudden, I'll realize that I haven't said anything to anyone for a long time. They know what I am doing. I know by the look on my wife's face when she has just received something from the Lord by meditating the Word. I want to hear it! I don't want her to quote something that just sounds pretty. I want to know if she has found something that we can act on and prosper. Meditation in the Word is so valuable!

Walking in truth is your responsibility. He said that as you follow that which is good and you walk in truth, then you will have prosperity of the soul. Once your soul begins to prosper, then financial, material, and physical prosperity cannot help but come to you, praise God!

10
Learn To Act, Talk, And Think Like God

A Christian whose soul is converted will learn to act, talk, and think like God. You may think that is a strong statement, and you will probably ask, "How in the world am I going to learn to act, talk, and think like God? Where am I going to find the information necessary to learn to think like Him? Do I study Commentaries? Listen to Theological sermons?" *NO!*

As I have been emphasizing throughout every chapter in this book: *it is all in God's Word.*

"The Bible?"

Yes, the Bible. Some people think that the Bible should lie on the coffee table for other people to see it. It is more than an ornament, a dust collector, or a place to store the flowers that you received from your first date or senior prom. I heard a story once, and I believe it illustrates what I am saying. Back during the depression, some people became so desperate that they started stealing. One man went to market and sold his produce for a sum of money. He thought, "Now where in the world am I going to hide this money, where nobody will find it?" He decided to hide it in the Bible, because that was the most unlikely place for anyone to look. Nobody ever thought of looking in the Bible. It was just another book as far as many people thought, so why bother reading it.

You say, "Do you mean to tell me that reading, studying, and meditating the Bible will enable me to think like God? Will this enable me to act and to talk like God?" It certainly will. For you see, the Bible is the thoughts of God put into print.

The Bible is still the *number one best seller in the world* today. Preachers are not the only one who have a right to own a copy of God's Word. This is the purpose of the Bible: to get you to thinking like God thinks, You see, as I begin to read Scriptures like 3 John 2: "Beloved, I wish above all things that thou mayest prosper and be in health even as thy soul prospereth," then I begin to realize that before true prosperity can come to me, in the measure that God desires that I should have it, I am going to have to learn to think as God thinks. I am going to have to get my mind renewed. I am going to have to teach my mind to think the thoughts of God. Therefore, the most sensible thing to do, to get this working in my life, is start reading my Bible and meditating His Word.

Isn't it amazing that God had the Bible put into print so you could learn to think like Him? The moment that you begin to think like God, that you become converted in your soul, your mind will be renewed to God's way of thinking.

How you act in a moment of crisis will determine whether or not you have a prosperous soul. The moment a crisis or adverse circumstances come to you, what do you do? Do your emotions begin to run away with you? Do you begin to break out in a cold sweat? Do you keep hitting your head and scream, "What am I going to do?" If you do, then you need to get back into the Word. Don't stop meditating the Word until your mind is renewed.

Once your mind begins to be renewed to what God says about the problem, then your emotions will become controlled. Your will becomes conformed to God's will. You won't think thoughts like, "This tragedy must be God's will to teach me something," or, "God wrecked my car to prove that He loves me."

You will think thoughts like this: "No weapon that is formed against me shall prosper. . . This is the heritage of the servants of the Lord, and my righteousness is of Him," and "If God is for me, who can be against me?"

Someone says, "Oh, I'd love to be able to talk like that." It doesn't come by loving to be able to do it. It comes from getting in there and meditating God's Word.

I am still working on it day and night. I have a desire and a thirst in my heart and in my soul to know more about God than I know about any other individual on this earth. I want to know the way He thinks more than I want to know the thoughts of anybody else on this earth. The only way that I can do that is by fellowshipping with Him and abiding in His Word. I can't learn all I want to learn about Him, think and act like Him, and talk like Him, by watching television eight hours a day, reading nothing but the newspaper, and fellowshipping with a group of nonbelieving, negative people.

Somebody said, "Isn't this going to make us different from the rest of the world?"

Well! God called you "peculiar!" Praise God! When you lay hold of this, *you will become peculiar.* Because in the midst of a crisis, you are the only one who is stable, established and settled, not wavering.

One of the greatest things that I have learned about the man who has his soul converted is when a crisis or pressure comes against him, rather than it destroying him, that is when he excels! Did you ever see Jesus in a situation where He was under pressure, or in a crisis, and He yielded to it and failed? No! Every time there was pressure you could spot Jesus standing above the crowd, because He excelled.

THE PROSPEROUS SOUL HAS A DISTINGUISHING MARK

A distinguishing mark of one who is re-born and his soul is converted, is this: He excels under pressure; he rises above every problem. This only comes from spending much time in the Word. Don't ever think that you can spend too much time in the Word.

IT'S A LONG WAY DOWN TO THE BOTTOM

If you ever get to the point where you think, "All right! I have arrived. I don't need the Bible anymore." Look out, *it is a long way down.* This is what happens to many good God anointed and ordained preachers. They reach the point where they think, "I know it all!" Instead of thirsting after *the Word*, they thirst after *things*. Please do not misunderstand: God will gladly give His kids all things that pertain to life. But *He does not want things to become priority.* Wrong priorities have ruined many good ministers of the gospel, as well as other members of the Body of Christ.

Prosperity of the soul comes when the Believer gives God's Word first place in his life. He continues in the Word. He meditates the Word, and by doing this, he learns to act, talk, and think like God. He says what the Word says, he does what the Word says to do, and then he begins to think just like God.

11
The Key

Many people have a lot of confidence in the writings found in John 3:16, and have none in Matthew 6:33, "But seek ye first the kingdom of God, and his righteousness; and all these things shall be added unto you." Why? Because of a lack of teaching. The reason that *Baptist* believe so strongly in the *new birth*, is because they preach it constantly. *The Church of Christ* believe strongly in *water baptism*, because they preach it constantly. The *Pentecostals* believe strongly in *talking in tongues*, because they preach it constantly. If you keep hearing the same teaching over and over and over, you will develop your faith in that particular teaching. God will confirm the Word that is being preached.

If you preach *salvation*, folks are going to *get saved*. If you preach *healing*, they are going to *get healed*. If you preach financial prosperity, they are going to be blessed financially.

Some time ago, I was in a meeting where the people who invited me specifically requested that I teach on the laws of prosperity. I had something else that I wanted to teach, but they said, "No, our people must have this teaching."

I asked the Lord what He thought about it, and He said, "They are right. They must hear this."

I thought, "Well, Lord, You know how people are. Some people are so funny about this. They don't like to hear preachers talking about money."

I was that way before I received the Lord. Every preacher I heard was either begging for money, or talking about how little of it he had. I didn't like that. I said, "That's the last time I'm going. I have heard those preachers begging for money all I want to hear! *They won't get any of mine!* I worked hard for it, and that preacher sits around all day and just eats and sleeps. Then he comes in the church, looks sad, tells all those hard luck stories, and all he wants is my money."

I remember one time in 1968, while I was on active duty, stationed in Fort Dix, New Jersey, a preacher went to our hometown to hold a series of meetings. My wife went to every meeting. One night, after I had just gotten off duty, I was sitting around with a bunch of guys playing cards. My wife called me long distance, and said, "Jerry, I just gave the most money in the offering that I have ever given in my life!"

I thought, "Whoopie!"

She said, "I wrote the preacher a check for $150." Oh, that made me mad. I had to play cards two nights in a row to win all that back! I had sold my favorite *hot-rod* to give her money to live on while I was gone, and she had taken $150 out of my *hot-rod money* to give to that preacher. That made me hot! That was a long time ago!

I now realize that the reason the Body of Christ has suffered financially, is because of the lack of teaching concerning the truth about financial prosperity.

THE MESSAGE OF VICTORY IS THE MESSAGE FOR THE HOUR

The message of victory is the message that is going to reach the multitudes in the last days. Where are the multitudes? They are watching their televisions. Television is going to be taken over by God. Men of faith are going to have prime time to preach the Word of faith. I am convinced that the men of God who are preaching the uncompromising message of God's Word will be able to go into television studios all over the United States, and anywhere else that God instructs, and preach the message of victory without hinderance! Do you know how much money this will take? If they say, "We don't have any time for you," then we will be so blessed that we will buy the station and make time for ourselves. It's coming! How do I know? Because God will give us power to get wealth in order that He may establish his Word in the earth. (Deut. 8:18)

Christians have suffered because of carnal thinking where *Prosperity* is concerned. It is time for them to know the truth and to walk in it. Most Christians do not know that it is God's will that they prosper. They will say, "Yes, I know that the Bible says that if we ask anything according to God's will, it shall be done. . . . But how do I know that I am praying according to the will of God?"

You have to allow *your will* to become conformed to *God's will.* Although we have touched on this in another chapter, I want you to get this in your spirit. As you learn to walk in truth and to meditate the Word of God, *your will* becomes conformed to *God's will.* When *your will* is conformed to *God's will,* you do not *will* to do anything that God wouldn't want you to do. You won't pray out of lust. You will always pray according to the Word and according to the will of God. That is the reason the Bible says, ". . . and it shall be given unto you of my Father which is in heaven."

Why?

Because God's Word is abiding in you, and you are abiding in Him. When you are abiding in Him, His will is abiding in you and you will never ask for anything that is not the will of God. That is what releases spiritual law.

Somebody said, "Well, I am praying that God will break my will." Well, quit praying that, because God doesn't want broken wills. A Christian with a *broken will* is absolutely useless where the kingdom of God is concerned.

God wants Christians who have *strong wills, conformed to His will.* I'm not talking about a strong *self-will,* a person in which everything is governed by what he thinks. I am talking about a will that is governed by what God thinks. Men and women of God who allow their wills to be conformed to God's will, are *strong willed* people. They will not fail. They *will* not to be beaten. They are uncompromising where their faith is concerned.

JESUS WAS VERY UNCOMPROMISING WHERE HIS FAITH WAS CONCERNED

Jesus did not allow circumstances to persuade or influence Him. He did not yield to pressure. He was very *strong willed.* One of the most beautiful scenes in the ministry of Jesus is when He prayed unto the Father God, and the Bible says that He was under such pressure that His sweat was as drops of blood. Jesus said, "Father, if there be any other way, let this cup pass from me; but *not my will, but Thine.*" Jesus' *will* was conformed to God's. Had He not conformed His *will* to God's, salvation for humanity would not have come.

Once Jesus prayed, He set His face — like flint, to go to Calvary. Peter tried to talk Jesus out of it, but Jesus said, "Get thee behind me satan." He wasn't calling Peter "satan", he was telling the devil, "My will has been conformed to God's will, and it doesn't matter what you say, I am going to the cross." Jesus wasn't blinded, He knew what was going to happen to Him when He got to Calvary. That is why He had prayed, "Father, if there be any other way, let it pass. . ." But when He realized that there was no other way, He said, "Not my will but Thine be done." Peter couldn't stop Him. The soldiers couldn't stop Him. Pilate couldn't stop Him, and Pilate's wife couldn't stop Him. She was willing. They wanted to wash their hands of the whole ordeal, but Jesus had set His face, *like flint*, and *He had set His will to perform the will of God*. There was no stopping Him. It was Calvary and nothing less. When He hung at Calvary and cried out, "It is finished," that was the testimony of a *strong willed man conformed to God's will*.

Jesus was prosperous in His ministry. He was not a failure. Everything that Jesus has is available to us. First Corinthians 2:16 tells us that *we have the mind of Christ*. We are capable of becoming as He is. Jesus said, ". . . as My Father hath sent me, even so send I you." (John 20:21)

WHAT IS THE KEY THAT UNLOCKS THE DOOR TO PROSPERITY

"Even as thy soul prospereth." This is the key. When John said, "Beloved, I wish (pray, desire) above all things that thou mayest prosper and be in health, even as thy soul prospereth," I am convinced that he was revealing God's will for us. I have said this in every chapter, and I shall keep on saying it. Even though it is the will of God that we prosper and be in health, it does not come on us just because we are believers. It is conditional, just as salvation is conditional. Salvation has been made available to every individual, but every individual has not received it. Every individual has not met the condition. The condition is, "That if thou shalt confess with thy mouth the Lord Jesus, and shalt believe in thine heart that God hath raised Him from the dead, thou shalt be saved." (Romans 10:9)

Righteousness has been made available to every person on earth, but all of them have not met the condition. In other words, even though all the promises of God are for every individual in the world, everybody in the world is not going to receive them, because they will not all meet the conditions.

The condition for living prosperously and in health is, "I wish that you prosper and be in health EVEN AS YOUR SOUL PROSPERS. The words *EVEN AS* are the key words. If you renew your mind to the Word of God, then your soul shall prosper. As your soul prospers, then you will prosper physically, materially, and financially. The words "EVEN AS" mean *in direct proportion to*. So you will always prosper in direct proportion to the prosperity of your soul.

12
Adam, The Image Of God

The Bible tells us in the first chapter of Genesis, that God created man in His image. "And God said, Let us make man in our image, after our likeness: and let them have dominion over the fish of the sea, and over the fowl of the air, and over the cattle, and over all the earth, and over every creeping thing that creepeth upon the earth. So God created man in His own image; male and female created he them" (vv. 26,27). We read in chapter 2:7-9, "And the Lord God formed man out of the dust of the ground, and breathed into his nostrils the breath of life; and man became a living soul. And the Lord God planted a garden eastward in Eden; and there he put the man whom he had formed. And out of the ground made the Lord God to grow every tree that is pleasant to the sight, and good for food; the tree of life also in the midst of the garden, and the tree of knowledge of good and evil." Notice: it does not say, "tree of good and evil." It says, "the tree of knowledge of good and evil." There is a difference.

ADAM WAS NOT A ROBOT!

Adam was there before Almighty God, and God breathed the breath of life into him. At that exact moment God caused the switch to be turned on inside Adam. He became alive; he became alert. God gave him the ability and the right to think — as soon as He would give him something to think about. Adam had the ability to talk as soon as God would give him something to talk about, and he had the ability to choose or to use his will as soon as God would put forth two choices to him. However, Adam was in an infant stage, so far as knowledge was concerned. As he stood there, he waited for God to say something so that he could think, speak, and use his will.

The beautiful thing about it was, God didn't create a robot. God gave Adam a will. He could believe in God his Creator, or he could turn his back on Him and choose his own destiny. There is not another creature that God created, in which He gave the ability that He gave to man.

ADAM WASN'T THE FIRST TO SIN

Many of us have thought that Adam was the first being who sinned. If no one had sinned, or if there had been no evil before Adam came, then why was there a tree of knowledge of *good and evil?* Lucifer, who was originally the anointed cherub of God, sinned first. The Bible says that he was beautiful and perfect in all of his ways until *iniquity* was found in him. Lucifer decided that because of his beauty and brightness, all of the angels should worship him like they were worshipping God. He tried to exalt himself above the most High God. It was then that he became a fallen angel, and his name was changed to Satan.

The fruit on the *tree of knowledge of good and evil* represented the seed of evil that was in Lucifer. God put it in the garden.

Some say, "Well, why did God put that tree in there? Didn't God know that man would want to check into it?"

We need to understand that evil had already taken place. *There was knowledge of evil as well as of good.* It would not have been right for God to hide that knowledge from Adam. He had already said, "Let us make man in our likeness, and in our image. . ." God had knowledge of the tree and since Adam was made in His likeness, God would not hide that knowledge from Adam. God is showing here that He had given man a unique position. He was God's *under-ruler* in the earth. Genesis 1:28 told us that God told Adam, ". . . multiply, subdue, and have dominion . . ." We can see God leading Adam around in the garden. He had already breathed the breath of life into him. We read in 2:15, "And the Lord God took the man, and put him into the garden to dress it and to keep it."

You don't see where Adam said, "Oh, but God, You don't understand. I'm so unworthy and I don't deserve all of this." Adam didn't know how to think or talk like that. He didn't know how to think in terms of defeat or failure, because he did not know what defeat or failure was. You don't see Adam, in the first couple of chapters of Genesis, walking up to God and saying, "You know, I feel like I am taking the flu." He had no knowledge of the *flu*. At that time all Adam knew was that his position was to dress the garden, subdue the earth, multiply and replenish it. Notice here, Adam was gaining some knowledge. God was feeding his mental computer. "And the Lord God commanded the man, saying, Of every tree of the garden thou mayest freely eat" (v.16). Adam knew that he could freely eat of every tree of the garden. "But of the tree of the knowledge of good and evil, thou shalt not eat of it: for in the day that thou eatest thereof thou shalt surely die" (v. 17). God had given Adam some instructions. "Adam, dress the garden, keep it, subdue it, have dominion over it, multiply, and replenish. You can freely eat of all the trees of the garden, BUT don't eat of the tree of the knowledge of good and evil. If you do, you will surely die."

The word *die* means separation from God. If you are separated from God you are separated from His knowledge. God is saying here, that this man, who had become a living soul, would die a spiritual death if he disobeyed God. This word *die*, in the Bible, never means "cease to exist." God is actually saying, "Adam, I can't hide this from you because it is something that has already taken place. There is the knowledge of good and evil. *The fruit of that tree represents the bad seed that was found in Lucifer many years ago.* I can't hide it from you, but I can tell you this: you can eat of anything in this garden except *the tree of the knowledge of good and evil.* If you disobey, *it will separate us and your soul will be flooded with evil knowledge."*

Everything was fine so far. Adam knew that he was not supposed to eat of that tree, and he knew why. But since Adam was not a robot, he had a choice. God made him a living soul. He gave him the ability to think. He gave him the knowledge that was necessary to live like God while he was in the earth, but Adam decided to disobey.

13
Adam Had Two Sources Of Knowledge

Have you ever told one of your children, "Now listen, Sweetheart, I don't want you playing in that refrigerator out there in the garage. That thing is dangerous. If that door shuts on you, you could die in there?" That is just like saying to some kids, "Go get in it, and see . . ." Everytime they walk by that refrigerator, it's tempting.

Adam was like that. He had been told, "Here is the tree of knowledge of good and evil, and if you partake of it, you will surely die." Don't you know that while Adam was out there naming all the animals, that every time he passed by that tree, it made him curious?

SO — GOD GAVE ADAM A HELP MEET: A STABILIZER

We are told in chapter two that Adam named all the living creatures, and we read, ". . . but for Adam there was not found an *help meet* for him. And the Lord God caused a deep sleep to fall upon Adam, and he slept: and He took one of his ribs, and closed up the flesh instead thereof; And the rib, which the Lord God had taken from man, made he a woman, and brought her unto the man" (vv. 20-22). God realized that Adam was having trouble there, and He created *a help meet — a stabilizer* for Adam. Eve's position was to be a *stabilizer for Adam.*

Every good wife is a *stabilizer* for her husband. There have been times when I knew what God wanted me to do, but at the same time I would be tempted to compromise. My wife knew what was happening on the inside of me. I would say, "Carolyn, I know what God wants me to do," but I would entertain the thought of compromising. But it never failed, my *stabilizer* always rose to the occasion, and said exactly what I needed to hear when I needed to hear it. She would stabilize me to the point that compromising no longer became a temptation.

WIVES SHOULD FULFILL THEIR ROLES AS STABILIZERS FOR THEIR HUSBANDS

We wouldn't have nearly the problems with men having affairs with other women if more wives were fulfilling their roles as *stabilizers* in the home.

I shall never forget once when I was in a meeting in Fort Worth. Brother Kenneth Copeland was ministering, and my wife and I were sitting in the audience. A preacher came down the aisle, and he was dressed very nicely. His wife followed behind him. That was the saddest looking woman I have ever seen, *so pale and washed-out looking*.

It didn't take me long to figure out why they didn't walk side by side. They sat down right across the aisle from us. Every time a young woman walked down the aisle to sit down, that man almost fell out of his chair, looking at them.

I thought, "Dear Lord! If his wife would make herself presentable and put on something attractive, he wouldn't be looking at all those other women." If she would fulfill her role as his stabilizer, he would not be so tempted to look at other women with a lustful attitude.

A NEW SOURCE OF KNOWLEDGE FOR ADAM

Since God had made Adam a living soul, he now had the knowledge necessary for him to live like God while he was here on earth. God knew what He was doing when He gave Eve to Adam as an *help meet* (stabilizer). Adam failed at his job and Eve failed at hers! They both partook of the fruit of the tree of knowledge of good and evil, and as a result they were separated from God. They died a spiritual death, their natures changed. Adam used his will and chose to eat of that tree, and as a result, his soul was flooded with the knowledge of evil.

Adam now had access to information from *a new source*, satan — the originator of iniquity. Now he could receive a new kind of knowledge. He was separated from God. From that time forward, things became so drastic that the Bible tells us that the thoughts and imaginations of mankind were continually on evil. God had to destroy all of the human race with the exception of Noah and his family. He had a plan that would enable Him to fill the earth with His knowledge once again.

14
God's Covenant With Man

Because Adam disobeyed God, and ate of the tree of the knowledge of good and evil, he became separated from God. He died a spiritual death and the thoughts of his new *god, satan*, caused his soul to become flooded with evil. Since that day, the Bible says that mankind became increasingly evil. "And God saw that the wickedness of man was great in the earth, and that every imagination of the thoughts of his heart was only evil continually" (Genesis 6:5).

GOD NEEDED ANOTHER AVENUE IN ORDER TO REACH MAN

God repented of making man (v.6), and because of the carnal, evil knowledge that filled man's soul, He decided to destroy the human race (with the exception of Noah and his family. "Noah found grace in the eyes of the Lord").

A LEGAL CONTRACT

Because of the disobedience of Adam, God had to deal with *spiritually dead people*, and it became necessary for Him to create a new avenue in order to get His Word in their minds. He found a man by the name of *Abram*, whom He later called "Abraham," who was willing to obey

His Word. God said, "And when Abram was ninety years old and nine, the Lord appeared to Abram, and said unto him, I am the Almighty God; walk before me, and be thou perfect. And I will make my covenant between me and thee, and will multiply thee exceedingly" (Genesis 17:1-2). God began to establish a legal contract with Abraham so that He could get His Word, His knowledge, His wisdom, and His thoughts back into the minds of men.

The purpose of the Old Covenant was to lead men out of their vanity and to teach them to think like God.

There was a problem: He was not dealing with men like Adam was before he fell. Before Adam fell he had the life and nature of God. Adam was not spiritually dead until he sinned. Then all mankind was born spiritually dead; they were *lorded over by satan.* God said, "For this is the covenant that I will make with the house of Israel after those days, saith the Lord; I will put my laws into their mind, and write them in their heart, and I will be to them a God, and they shall be to me a people" (Hebrews 8:10). Jesus' purpose in coming to earth was to break the power of satan over mankind, so that man could once again be in the position that Adam was before he sinned. Man could once again have the life of God on the inside. Not only that, but God said through the mouth of Jesus, "When I leave, I will send you another Comforter. He will not only be with you, but he will be in you." He also gave us a copy of His Word. The Christian has the Holy Spirit living on the inside to teach him; he has a copy of the Word of God so that he can read it and understand the mind of God. All he has to do is read it and meditate it. Then he will begin to think like God, and it will be well with him.

He went on to say in the Word that, "We have the mind of Christ." We, as Christians, stand in a beautiful position today. Not only are we filled with the nature of God, but we have the Holy Spirit living on the inside of us, teaching the Word of God to us. Where Adam could only receive God's knowledge when he walked and talked with Him in the *cool of the day*, we don't have to wait until the *cool of the day*. We have Him inside us; we can hear His voice twenty-four hours a day. Praise God! We can hear His voice.

God desires that our minds become renewed, our wills conformed to His will, our emotions controlled by His Word, and our thinking faculties selective thinking on good things, honest things, and on things that are lovely and of a good report. As this takes place, then prosperity comes.

15
Some Prosperous Souls

You have read in the third chapter of the book of Daniel about a king by the name of Nebuchadnezzar, who sent out a decree to all the inhabitants of the land. When the instruments of music sounded all the inhabitants of the land were to fall down and worship, according to the king's decree. If they refused to do so, they would be cast into a *fiery furnace*.

We read in verse 12 where one of the king's captains came to him and said, "There are certain Jews whom thou hast set over the affairs of the province of Babylon, Shadrach, Meshach, and Abednego; these men, O king, have not regarded thee: they serve not thy gods, nor worship the golden image which thou hast set up." Verse 13 says, "Then Nebuchadnezzar in his rage and fury commanded to bring Shadrach, Meshach, and Abednego. Then they brought these men before the King." You will remember that the king asked them why they did not fall down and worship the golden image at the sound of the instruments of music. I want you to notice how they answered him. "Shadrach, Meshach, and Abednego answered and said to the king, O Nebuchadnezzar, we are not careful to answer thee in this matter. If it be so, our God whom we serve is able to deliver us from the burning fiery furnace, and he will deliver us out of thine hand, O king. But if not, be it known unto thee, O king, that we will not serve thy gods, nor worship the golden image which thou hast set up" (vv. 16-18).

You will remember that Adam was told, that if he partook of that tree he would surely die. Adam had two choices, and he chose the wrong one. And here — these three Hebrew children were standing in the same position in which Adam had stood. They had two sources of knowledge that they could act upon. The law had already been given at that time, and the law said, "Thou shalt worship the Lord thy God, and Him only shalt thou serve." That was the knowledge of God. They had God's knowledge in their thinking. They had it in their hearts, and they had it in their souls.

On the other hand the king had *come up* with another knowledge. "If you don't bow down and worship this image, you will be cast into the fiery furnace and you will die."

Just as Adam had two choices, these three men also had two choices. But unlike Adam, they had prosperous souls. They said, "We choose God's knowledge." They may not have been very large or tall in stature, but know this, if you find a man who has his mind set that it is God's way, or no way, he becomes a giant — where God is concerned. Those men were giants, praise God! They were saying, "We will not yield to this carnal knowledge; we will not turn our backs on the knowledge our God has given us, and we will not serve your *gods.*"

NEBUCHADNEZZAR GOT HOT AND SO DID THE FURNACE!

That furnace got seven times hotter than it had ever been before. In fact, it was so hot that the flames engulfed the men who were to throw the three Hebrew men into the furnace, and slew them. Verse 23 says, "And these three men Shadrach, Meshach, and Abednego, *fell down bound into the midst of the fiery furnace."*

The king thought that would be the end of them. But if you will read on, you will find that *the king got a "shocker!"* He looked into the furnace and saw four men, instead of three! He said, "Didn't we throw three men bound into the furnace?"

"That's right!" they said.

The king then said, ". . . Lo, I see four men loose, walking in the midst of the fire, and they have no hurt; and the form of the fourth is like the Son of God" (v.25).

WHAT HAPPENED

Those men had prosperous souls. They refused to bow their knees to that heathen king. They chose to keep God's knowledge.

God's knowledge is, "Beloved, I desire that you prosper and be in health EVEN AS your soul prospers." *Prosperity comes in direct proportion to the prosperity of your soul.*

If you will read the rest of the account in Daniel 3, you will find that the king pulled them out of that *fiery furnace,* and their coats were not even burned; their hair was not singed, and they didn't even have the smell of smoke on them.

Somebody said, "Oh, the trial they went through!" Do you call that "a trial?" They came out smelling like roses.

The king said, "Blessed be the God of these men . . ." And we read in verses 29-30: "Therefore I make a decree, that every people, nation, and language, which speak any thing amiss against the God of Shadrach, Meshach, and Abednego, shall be cut in peices, and their houses shall be made a dunghill: because there is no other God that can deliver after this sort. Then the king promoted Shadrach, Meshach, and Abednego, in the province of Babylon." The word *promoted,* in the Hebrew, means "made to prosper."

They were made to prosper because their souls prospered. They refused to go against the knowledge of God. Their minds were renewed to what God said. Their wills were conformed to God's will, and they had their emotions under control.

They were not born-again men, but they had prosperous souls.

Shadrach, Meshach, and Abednego thought only the thoughts of God. They willed to do God's will, and they had their emotions under control. They had prosperous souls. If these men could have prosperous souls how much more can a born again, Spirit filled, believer, who has a copy of everything that God said, have a prosperous soul?

Those men could not turn over to the Book of Romans and see what chapter 12 says. Romans 12 had not been written yet!

You may ask, "Well, how did they get their souls to prosper?"

God put His Word in their minds and wrote it in their hearts. That is exactly what the Bible is for. That is the reason that the Holy Ghost came. You are to put God's Word in your mind and write it in your heart, so you can think like God. Any Christian who thinks like God is not a failure.

You may ask, "How can I prosper in my soul?"

Well, I'll tell you this: Your soul must thirst after the Word of God. Psalm 42:2 says, "My soul thirsteth for God, for the living God: when shall I come and appear before God?" It must be an act of your will. You don't prosper in your soul by wishing that you can. You must desire God's Word more than you desire anything else. Your soul must thirst after the living God. I like the way Psalm 63:8 puts it, "My soul followeth hard after thee . . ." This fellow is not getting behind. He is following hard after the Word of God. Psalm 25:1 says, "Unto thee, O Lord, do I lift up my soul." That is exactly what Romans 12:1,2 tells us to do: "I beseech you therefore, brethren, by the mercies of God, that ye present your bodies a living sacrifice, holy, acceptable unto God, which is your reasonable service. And be not conformed to this world: but be ye transformed by the renewing of your mind, that ye may prove what is that good, and acceptable, and perfect will of God."

The psalmist was saying, "I am lifting up my soul, unto You, Oh God." And that is what the New Testament is telling us to do. *Your body is the physical housing of your soul.* If you will present it unto God, and not be conformed to this world, but get your mind renewed to God's Word, you will prosper.

Paul says in Ephesians 4:23, "And be renewed in the spirit of your mind." Isaiah 1:19 says, "If ye be willing and obedient, ye shall eat the good of the land." If you are willing and obedient, you will eat the good of the land; drive it, wear it, and live it. *Be willing and obedient. That is where the action comes in.* If you are willing and obedient, and you are following hard after the Word of God *Prosperity of the Soul is available unto you.*

Jesus paid a precious price for the prosperity of our souls. Today — believers stand in a unique position, because of what God has made available to us.

If you are born again, filled with His nature, you have the mind of Christ; you have the Holy Ghost in you as your teacher, and you have a copy of God's Word. There is no reason for you, or any believer in the earth today to fail.

"Beloved, I wish (desire) *above all things* that thou mayest prosper and be in health, *even as thy soul prospereth.*"